THE WORLD AROUND ME

SHAPES

····· · IN MY WORLD ·····

Written by

Hermione Redshaw

KidHaven PUBLISHING

Published in 2023 by **KidHaven Publishing,
an Imprint of Greenhaven Publishing, LLC**
2544 Clinton St., Buffalo, NY 14224

© 2022 Booklife Publishing
This edition is published by arrangement with
Booklife Publishing

Written by: Hermione Redshaw
Edited by: William Anthony
Illustrated by: Amy Li

Font (cover, page 1) courtesy of cuppuccino on
Shutterstock.com. With thanks to Getty Images,
Thinkstock Photo and iStockphoto.

Cataloging-in-Publication Data

Names: Redshaw, Hermione, author. I Li, Amy,
illustrator.
Title: Shapes in my world / by Hermione Redshaw,
illustrated by Amy Li.
Description: New York : KidHaven Publishing, 2023.
I Series: The world around me
Identifiers: ISBN 9781534543386 (pbk.) I
ISBN 9781534543409 (library bound) I
ISBN 9781534543416 (ebook)
Subjects: LCSH: Shapes--Juvenile literature.
Classification: LCC QA445.5 R394 2023 I
DDC 516.15--dc23

Manufactured in the United States of America

CPSIA compliance information: Batch #CWKH23
For further information contact Greenhaven Publishing LLC
at 1-844-317-7404.

Please visit our website, www.greenhavenpublishing.com.
For a free color catalog of all our high-quality books,
call toll free 1-844-317-7404 or fax 1-844-317-7405.

Find us on

Dylan knows all about shapes!
He sees shapes everywhere.

The wheels on Dylan's bike are circles. Circles are round.

Circle wheels roll.

Dylan adds **square** wheels.

The bike does not move.

The roof on Dylan's house
is a **triangle**.

Triangles have
three straight sides.

Rain falls on the roof.

The rain slides down the sides.

Dylan's door is a **rectangle.**

Dylan can walk through it.

Dog doors are square.

Only dogs can walk through them.

Bees live
in hives.

Their hives are
covered in shapes.

These shapes are hexagons.

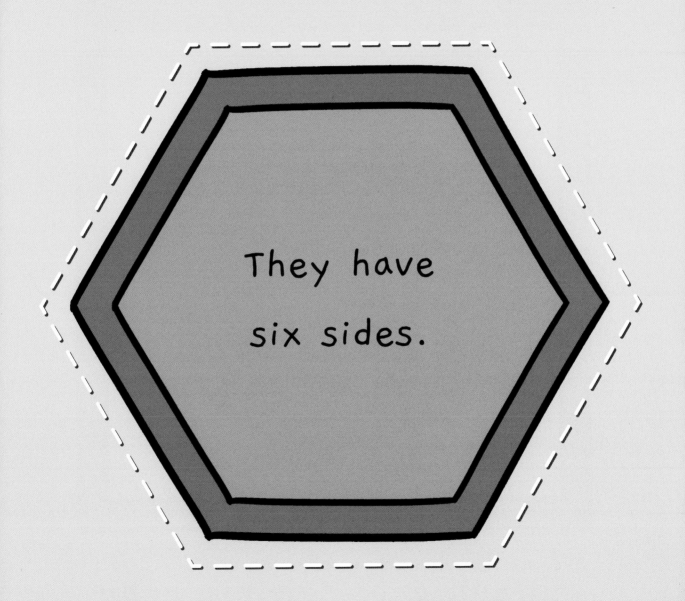

They have
six sides.

Dylan's mirror is square.

He can only see his head.

This mirror is a rectangle.

Dylan can see all of him!

Watermelons are round.

They roll around the table.

A slice of watermelon has one round side and one straight side.

The refrigerator
is a
rectangle.

It does
not move.

Sometimes the moon is a circle.

Sometimes it is not.

A crescent has
two curved sides.

Bananas are crescent shapes.

Dylan draws stars.

His stars have five points.

The stars in the sky look small.

Do they look like Dylan's stars?

Dylan has round glasses.

Dylan's mom has square glasses.

They both look great!